LIGHTNING
BOLT
BOOKS™

Explore Jupiter

Liz Milroy

Lerner Publications ◆ Minneapolis

PAGE PLUS

Scan the QR code on page 21 to see Jupiter in 3D!

Lerner Publications Company
An imprint of Lerner Publishing Group, Inc.
241 First Avenue North
Minneapolis, MN 55401 USA

For reading levels and more information, look up this title at www.lernerbooks.com.

Main body text set in Billy Infant regular.
Typeface provided by SparkType.

Editor: Brianna Kaiser
Lerner team: Sue Marquis

Library of Congress Cataloging-in-Publication Data

Names: Milroy, Liz, author.
Title: Explore Jupiter / Liz Milroy.
Other titles: Lightning bolt books. Planet explorer.
Description: Minneapolis, MN : Lerner Publications, 2021 | Series: Lightning bolt books - Planet explorer | Includes bibliographical references and index. | Audience: Ages 6-9 | Audience: Grades 2-3 | Summary: "Find out what makes Jupiter different from other planets in this scientific exploration. Readers will learn about the planet's weather, moons, space missions, and more"— Provided by publisher.
Identifiers: LCCN 2020013927 (print) | LCCN 2020013928 (ebook) | ISBN 9781728404097 (library binding) | ISBN 9781728418452 (ebook)
Subjects: LCSH: Jupiter (Planet)—Juvenile literature.
Classification: LCC QB661 .M553 2021 (print) | LCC QB661 (ebook) | DDC 523.45—dc23

LC record available at https://lccn.loc.gov/2020013927
LC ebook record available at https://lccn.loc.gov/2020013928

Manufactured in the United States of America
1-48467-48981-6/3/2020

Table of Contents

All about Jupiter

A huge storm called the Great Red Spot surrounds you. You're on Jupiter! It is the biggest planet in our solar system.

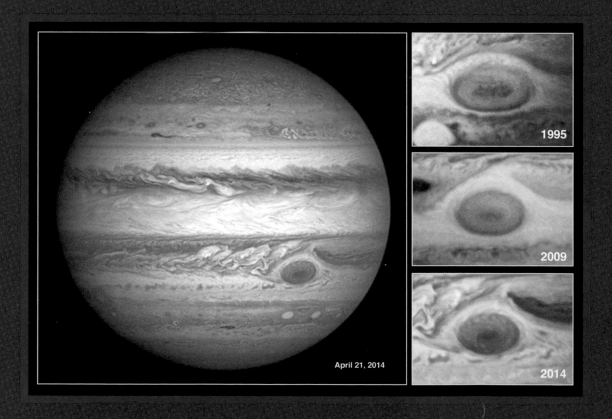

April 21, 2014

1995

2009

2014

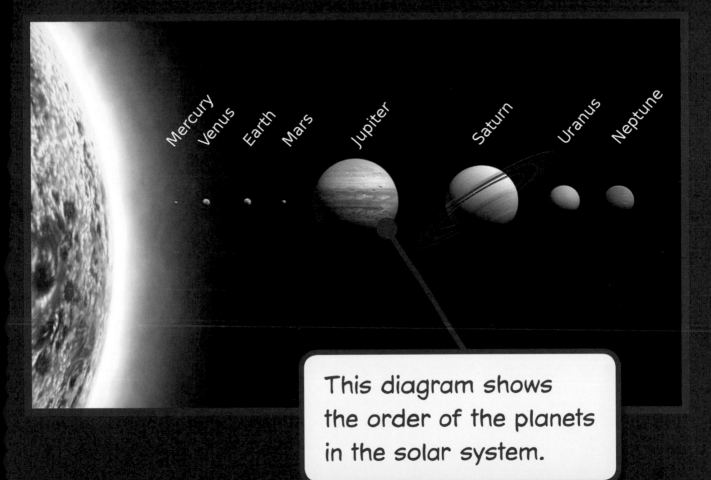

Mercury Venus Earth Mars Jupiter Saturn Uranus Neptune

This diagram shows the order of the planets in the solar system.

Jupiter is the fifth planet from the sun. It's about 484 million miles (779 million km) away from the sun.

Jupiter is called a gas giant because it is very big and made mostly of gas. If you put Jupiter on one end of a seesaw, it would take 318 Earths to balance it out on the other end.

This image shows how large Jupiter is compared to Earth.

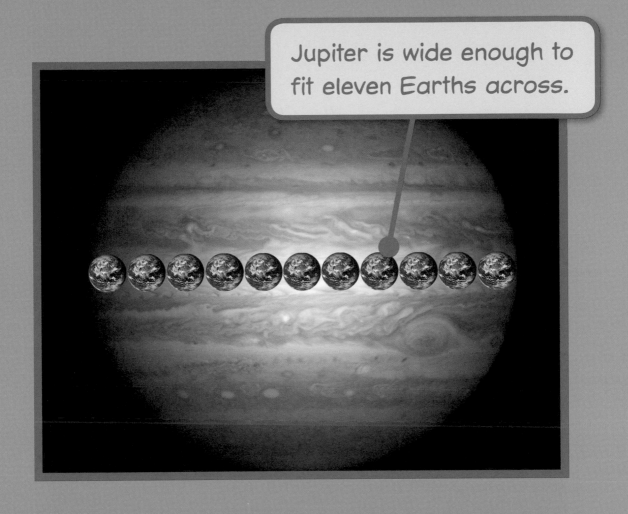

Jupiter is wide enough to fit eleven Earths across.

Jupiter is 88,846 miles (142,984 km) across. That's more than eleven times the width of Earth. If Earth were a little smaller than a grape, Jupiter would be the size of a basketball.

Jupiter's Moons

Earth has only one moon, but Jupiter has many more. There are seventy-nine known moons around Jupiter.

People can use a telescope to see Jupiter's biggest moons from Earth.

Jupiter's four biggest and most famous moons are called Io, Europa, Ganymede, and Callisto. They can be seen from Earth with telescopes.

Ganymede is the largest moon in our solar system. It is 3,272 miles (5,268 km) across. It's even bigger than planet Mercury.

Ganymede appears behind Jupiter.

Jupiter and its moons are named after figures in ancient Roman and Greek mythology. Ancient Romans named Jupiter after a god because it looked very bright in the night sky.

Living on Jupiter

Jupiter wouldn't be a nice place to visit. Its winds can blow almost twice as fast as Earth's hurricanes.

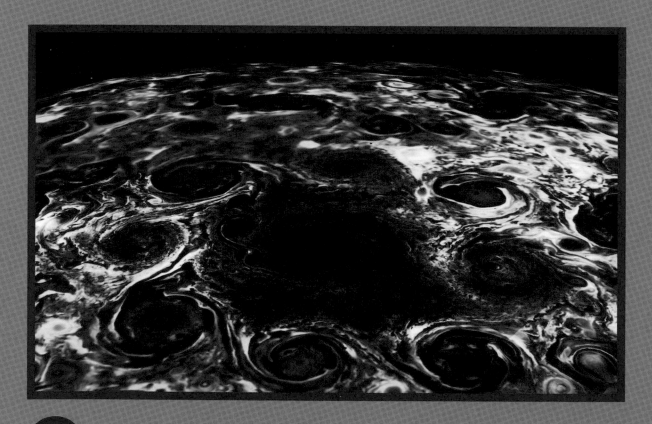

Some astronomers think Jupiter's surface might be solid metal. But it would be hard for a spacecraft to get past Jupiter's stormy sky and land there.

Jupiter's sky is full of storms like the Great Red Spot.

Jupiter is very cold. The average temperature on Jupiter is -234°F (-148°C).

Jupiter is much too cold for human life.

Other planets get most of their heat from the sun. But Jupiter heats up from its core. Under its thick, cold atmosphere, Jupiter's core can be very warm.

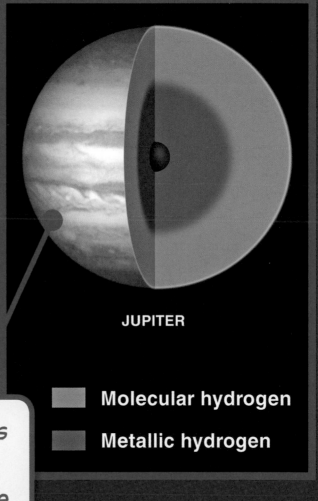

JUPITER

Molecular hydrogen

Metallic hydrogen

This diagram shows Jupiter's layers from its atmosphere to its core.

Checking Out Jupiter

Astronomers study Jupiter with spacecraft. Nine spacecraft have visited or flown past Jupiter. In the early 1970s, *Pioneer 10* and *Pioneer 11* became the first to fly by Jupiter.

Jupiter has faint rings.

In the late 1970s, *Voyager 1* and *Voyager 2* made a big discovery. They saw that Jupiter had rings made of dust.

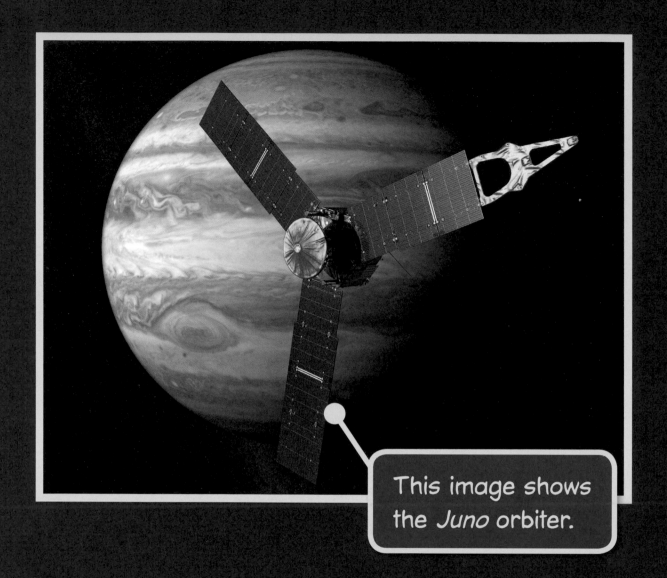

This image shows the *Juno* orbiter.

The *Juno* orbiter arrived at Jupiter in 2016. It is still in Jupiter's orbit. Astronomers continue to learn about Jupiter.

Future missions will try to see if any of Jupiter's moons have water. Could people live on Jupiter's moons one day? Maybe you'll be one of the scientists to find out!

Jupiter in view from its moon Europa

Planet Facts

- Gravity is a force that pulls things together. Jupiter's gravity is so strong that astronomers use it to help spacecraft go farther into space. Think of it as a giant slingshot!

- Sometimes Jupiter's poles light up with beautiful colors called auroras. On Earth, these are known as the northern lights.

- Jupiter spins so fast that each day takes only ten hours. But a year on Jupiter is 4,333 Earth days, or about twelve years.

Space Story

In the past, people thought that everything in the universe revolved around Earth. In 1610, Galileo Galilei looked at the night sky through a telescope. He saw four small objects moving around Jupiter. He called them starlets. His discovery helped prove that Earth wasn't the center of the universe. Astronomers later learned that the starlets were Jupiter's four largest moons.

Scan the QR code to the right to see Jupiter in 3D!

Glossary

astronomer: a scientist who looks at stars, planets, and other things in outer space

atmosphere: a layer of gas that surrounds a planet

core: the center of a planet

gas giant: a big planet that is made up mostly of gas

hurricane: a powerful storm with strong winds and rain

orbit: the path taken by one body circling around another body

solar system: our sun and everything that orbits around it

spacecraft: a ship made by people to move through space

telescope: a tool used to get a better look at objects in space

Learn More

Goldstein, Margaret J. *Discover Jupiter*. Minneapolis: Lerner Publications, 2019.

Milroy, Liz. *Explore Saturn*. Minneapolis: Lerner Publications, 2021.

NASA for Students
https://www.nasa.gov/stem/forstudents/k-4/index.html

NASA Space Place—All about Jupiter
https://spaceplace.nasa.gov/all-about-jupiter/en/

Nichols, Michelle. *Astronomy Lab for Kids: 52 Family-Friendly Activities*. Beverly, MA: Quarry, 2016.

Ready, Jet, Go! Planets in Our Solar System
https://pbskids.org/learn/readyjetgo/

Index

Photo Acknowledgments

Image credits: NASA/GSFC, p. 4; WP/Wikimedia Commons (CC BY-SA 3.0), p. 5; NASA/JPL/ Space Science Institute, p. 6; NASA/JPL, pp. 7, 18; NASA/JPL/DLR, p. 8;NPS/M.Quinn/flickr (CC BY 2.0), p. 9; NASA, ESA, and E. Karkoschka (University of Arizona), p. 10; The J. Paul Getty Museum, Los Angeles, p. 11; NASA/JPL-Caltech/SwRI/ASI/INAF/JIRAM, p. 12; NASA/JPL -Caltech/SwRI/MSSS/Joerg-Schneider, p. 13; NASA/JPL-Caltech/SwRI/MSSS/Kevin M. Gill/flickr (CC BY 2.0), p. 14; NASA/Lunar and Planetary Institute, p. 15; NASA/ARC, p. 16; NASA/Johns Hopkins University Applied Physics Laboratory/Southwest Research Institute, p. 17; NASA/JPL-Caltech, p. 19.

Cover: NASA, ESA, A. Simon (Goddard Space Flight Center), and M.H. Wong (University of California, Berkeley) (CC BY 4.0).